CHAMPION CITIZEN:

Courtesy *Sport* Magazine Dec. 1954

GEORGE TALIAFERRO
Finding the Champion in You!

Created by

Published and distributed by
in association with

IBJ Book Publishing
41 E. Washington St., Suite 200
Indianapolis, IN 46204
www.ibjbp.com

Copyright 2011 by Hamilton County Community Tennis Association.
ALL RIGHTS RESERVED. No part of this book, lesson plans, or educational activities associated with this book may be reproduced in any manner without the express written consent of Hamilton County Community Tennis Association. All inquiries should be made to Hamilton County Community Tennis Association.

HCCTA is grateful to the USTA Serves Foundation for its grant to make the *Champion Citizens Series One* a reality.

Cover photo: *Sport* Magazine December, 1954

HCCTA Elementary Reads logo design compliments of Fred Learey, a graphic arts student at Anderson University.

HCCTA is grateful to Susie Learey for donating her copy editing services.

HCCTA is grateful to the athletes and their representatives for their support and contributions to these books.

ISBN 978-1-934922-55-2
First Edition

Printed in the United States of America

Courtesy Helen Moser Petersen

This book is dedicated to people who don't let anything get in the way of their education and life goals and continue to smile at the world.

TABLE OF CONTENTS

1. SAVING FOR A FOOTBALL	1
2. KEEPING A PROMISE	2
3. HIGH SCHOOL FOOTBALL	3
4. COLLEGE FOOTBALL	5
5. U.S. ARMY	7
6. NFL FOOTBALL	8
7. HELPING OTHERS	9
VOCABULARY	11
FUN FACTS	13

CHAMPION CITIZEN:
GEORGE TALIAFERRO
Finding the Champion in You!

George (second from right) with his neighborhood friends in 1941.

1 SAVING FOR A FOOTBALL

When George Taliaferro was a boy, he and his friends wanted to play football. But they didn't have enough money to buy the ball. To earn the money, they **scoured** the neighborhood looking for aluminum cans and glass bottles that they could take to be recycled. After a lot of hard work, they got enough money to buy the neighborhood's first football.

Then came the even-harder decision: Who would get to keep it? After much discussion, they decided that George's house was in the middle of the neighborhood, where they could all easily get to it, so he got to keep it. He couldn't believe his good luck!

Series One of Books About **Inspirational Athletes**

George and his friends played football every day. If his friends weren't available, George would kick the ball in the air and catch it. This experience taught him a lot. He learned what he could **achieve** with hard work, and he learned about football. He grew to love the game.

2 KEEPING A PROMISE

One summer day when George was in grade school, his father asked him to dig out a garden in the backyard by the time he returned from work. Before George could start digging, some of his friends stopped by, asking him to go to the neighborhood pool. George couldn't resist the **temptation** of the cool water on such a hot day. He decided he had plenty of time to go swimming first and then dig the garden before his dad came home at four in the afternoon.

George being tackled in a game against the Baltimore Colts.

After swimming for a while, George lay down by the pool. He didn't mean to, but he fell asleep. When he woke up he asked the lifeguard what time it was. He was **shocked** to find out it was almost four already! He jumped up and ran as fast as he could. He was only home for a few minutes, though, before his dad arrived. He didn't have time to start digging.

His dad was **disappointed** in him. "A man is only as good as his word," he told George. In other words, he wanted his son to understand that it is very important to keep a promise. It upset George to disappoint his father, so he decided he would not stop digging until the garden was done. He grabbed a shovel and got started. He wasn't finished when it got dark, so his mother came outside and held a lantern for him while he worked.

George would never forget the **valuable** lesson he learned that day, that he should always keep a promise so others could trust him.

3 HIGH SCHOOL FOOTBALL

In 1941 George took that lesson with him to Gary Roosevelt High School in Gary, Indiana. By this time he and his friends had been playing football for years. George was getting good at it! He decided to play for his high school team, the Panthers.

When George was in high school, students were **separated** by the color of their skin. George had to go to an all-black high school because he was black. The black schools were not allowed to play against the white schools. They had to travel long distances — as far as Tennessee — in order to play games of football.

George with the Los Angeles Dons in 1949.

Champion Citizen: George Taliaferro

Luckily, today we know better than to separate people just because their skin is a different color. But it didn't matter where he played. George was always unstoppable when he was on the football field. George played many different positions, but he was mainly a quarterback.

There was one all-white school in East Chicago, Indiana, also named Roosevelt High School. The football coach understood that it was okay for his white players to play against black players. He asked George's coach if the Panthers would play against his team. The two coaches agreed and decided on the game time.

George and his teammates had never played a tougher team. The other team had won thirty-four games in a row and had won several state championships. George didn't let that stop him. He scored the touchdown that led his team to **victory**.

George and his teammates showed that blacks and whites could play together, and George showed that he was quickly becoming a football star.

Pete Rucinski, the East Chicago Roosevelt High School football coach, was so impressed with how George played against his team that he called Indiana University football coach Bo McMillin the very next morning. He told Coach McMillin what a great player George was and that he should have George play on his IU team.

Coach McMillin had never heard about George. No statistics were kept on black athletes. They were not eligible to be named to all-state teams or receive any other honors that the white players received.

Coach Rucinski said George was the best high school tailback in Indiana, but there was one problem. He was colored, meaning his skin was black. Coach McMillin said he did not care what George's skin color was — it could be purple. If George was as good as Coach Rucinski said, Coach McMillin wanted him to play at IU.

4 COLLEGE FOOTBALL

George went to Indiana University to earn a college degree. He knew playing football was the only way for him to earn a degree. Every day for eighteen years George's parents told him two things: "We love you. You must be educated."

George knew he could play against white players. He had done it once in high school, beating the best team in the state. Besides, "If they put their pants on one leg at a time, I'll do fine," George said. He meant that black people and white people were all the same. They do the same things.

George on the practice field at Indiana University at age eighteen in 1945.

When he got to IU, George became worried when he saw how big the other players were. He asked himself, "Should I really be here?" However, he didn't take long to fit in and become a star on IU's team, just like he had been in high school.

One of George's proudest moments was helping his team win the Old Oaken Bucket, a trophy given to the winner of the game between IU and Purdue. The two schools are huge **rivals**, so it was a big deal to win. In another game he scored three touchdowns against Minnesota.

Another favorite **accomplishment** was his team's winning the Big Ten Championship in 1945. It was the only time an Indiana University football team had an undefeated season, and the only time IU won the Big Ten Championship outright. George was the only African-American at IU to be named All-America for three years.

At Indiana University, George still had to face **challenges** with **racism** because he was black. He could not live on the campus. He could only go to the movies on certain days and had to sit in a certain area. He couldn't eat at any of the restaurants, even though there were pictures of him playing football on the walls of some of them.

As usual, George did not sit around complaining about it. He decided to do something. So he started fighting against racism. He was as good at that as he was at football. Pretty soon he was able to eat at the restaurants and sit in the theater. He was showing everyone that the color of your skin didn't matter and that you could overcome any challenges with hard work and **determination**.

5 U.S. ARMY

Due to George's strong impact on Indiana's football team, other college coaches were afraid to play them. It is **rumored** that one of the coaches got George **drafted** into the U.S. Army at the end of World War II so his team would not have to play against George that year.

George in the U.S. Army in 1946.

While he was in the army, George faced more racial challenges, since the army was not **integrated**. The white and black soldiers were separated. He had to face racism just like he did in high school and college.

Despite facing challenges like racism and leaving college, there was something good about being drafted into the army. George met Viola Jones, who would later become his wife.

Series One of Books About **Inspirational Athletes**

6 NFL FOOTBALL

George with the New York Yanks in 1950.

Courtesy George Taliaferro

George was only in the army for sixteen months, and then he went back to Indiana University. In 1949 a childhood dream came true — George was drafted by the Chicago Bears! Since George had lived so close to Chicago when he was growing up, the Chicago Bears were his favorite team.

However, when he got the call from the Bears, he had already told the Los Angeles Dons that he would play on their football team. Because no black man had EVER been drafted by the NFL before, George never dreamed the Chicago Bears would draft him.

Then George remembered what his father had said when he didn't dig the garden, "A man is only as good as his word." George wanted to play for the Chicago Bears more than anything, but he had made a promise to the Los Angles Dons. He had to keep his promise.

George was now playing NFL football, but he also continued to fight racism. He played professional football for seven years, playing for the Baltimore Colts, Dallas Texans, New York Yanks, Los Angeles Dons and Philadelphia Eagles. He played seven

Champion Citizen: George Taliaferro

positions in college and professional football — running back, quarterback, punter, punt returner, wide receiver, kickoff returner, and defensive cornerback. George could run, kick, and throw. He was, and still is, the only player to ever play seven positions in the NFL!

7 HELPING OTHERS

After his football career, George went back to college to earn another degree. He earned a graduate degree in social work from Howard University. He used his college degrees to help others. For awhile he was a social worker and helped prisoners find a way to live an honest life.

Judge Viola J. Taliaferro in 1989

After their four daughters were older, he supported his wife Viola when she decided to enter Indiana University School of Law. For three years George helped with his daughters and household chores so Viola could study. Viola became a lawyer and eventually one of Indiana's best judges for children and family law. She received many honors. George's helping with the family made it possible for Viola to succeed in her career.

George eventually ended up going back to Indiana University to work as a professor, where he inspired his students. He continued to work towards equal treatment for all people, and he helped many charities. His favorite charity is COTA — Children's Organ Transplant Association. Every year George has a golf tournament that helps raise money so children anywhere in the continental United States can have organ transplants that save their lives.

George's wife and four daughters. Left to right: Renee, Linda, Donna, Viola and Teri

George is an inspiration to everyone who faces obstacles and challenges. He is more than a champion football player. He is a champion **citizen**.

Now Find the Champion in You!

Accomplishment	Something done well.
Achieve	Accomplish a goal.
Challenges	Struggles.
Citizen	A person who makes his community better by doing good things for others.
Determination	A person's decision to do something.
Disappointed	Sad or displeased.
Drafted	Selected or chosen.
Integrate	Bring together.
Racism	Treating people badly because of their skin color.
Rivals	Competitors.
Rumored	Gossiped.
Scour	Look hard and long for something.
Separate	Keep apart from one another.
Shocked	Surprised or upset.
Temptation	A wish to do something, especially something foolish or unwise.
Valuable	Something that is worth a lot.
Victory	Success in a struggle or obstacle.

Series One of Books About **Inspirational Athletes**

George and Viola's wedding on November 24, 1950

George and author Dawn Knight at book signing at the NCAA Hall of Champions

George with former Indianapolis Colts coach Tony Dungy in 2010 when they received the Thomas A. Brady Sports Achievement Awards from The Methodist Sports Medicine/Orthopedic Specialists Research and Education Foundation.

George posing in his IU jersey and Viola in her judicial robe on August 7, 2011.

Champion Citizen: George Taliaferro